Published by Seacoast Press, an imprint of MindStir Media, LLC

1931 Woodbury Ave. #182 | Portsmouth, New Hampshire 03801 | USA

1.800.767.0531 | www.seacoastpress.com

Printed in the United States of America

ISBN-13: 978-0-9978612-8-0

Walking from HERE TO THERE

Finding My Way
ON EL CAMINO

Christy Day

DEDICATED TO

Hillary and Julia

Dearest daughters, lights of my life.
Your love and enthusiastic support of
my Pilgrimage made it inevitable.

TABLE OF *Contents*

INTRODUCTION

Whatever you can do or dream you can, begin it.
Boldness has genius, power, and magic in it.

~Goethe

I was originally inspired to walk El Camino by the movie, "The Way." I had never done a Pilgrimage and what I learned from the movie piqued my interest. Later, when I went to a presentation given by an American Pilgrim at my local Amherst, NH, library, I realized the Pilgrimage was doable. I was in. I spent the next year planning and dreaming. I walked faithfully with a friend. I bought my backpack and began making a pile of items to take. I bought the guidebook. I bought new shoes and socks. I started wearing my backpack on our walks. Above all, I started believing that I could do it and committed myself to figuring out what it took to succeed at this huge endeavor.

What I want to capture is the magic of the journey and the discipline required to sustain a 39-day Pilgrimage. I want to explore the fine art of making the right choices. I want to express the humor in putting up with instead of getting annoyed. I will delve into the joy of finding the balance between respect for others and their space and creating a space of my own. Explore with me the joy and fear, the daily delights, the connection with fellow Pilgrims.

My hope is that this book will help you reach for your stars. If you have no ambitions to walk El Camino, you can enjoy it vicariously with me. If you want to walk El Camino, perhaps this will inspire you to get planning. As Confucius said, "Wherever you go, go with all your heart."

Chapter 1

WHO IS ST. JAMES,
WHAT IS EL CAMINO,
WHY THIS PILGRIM ROUTE

To strive, to seek, to find, and to not yield.
~Alfred, Lord Tennyson

James is St. James the Great, son of Zebedee and Salome, brother of John, one of Christ's beloved Apostles. He is the patron saint of Spain and Portugal. There is historical evidence that he came to the Iberian Peninsula to convert pagans. He returned to Jerusalem and Herod beheaded him for his efforts in 42 A.D.

Legend, lore, and myth surround the return of his body to western Spain, and the stories involve scallop shells, which are the symbol of El Camino. His body is now coffered beneath the Cathedral of Santiago de Compostela. The Pilgrimage honors his martyrdom and sainthood. Myth tells us that he appeared on a white charger in 844 to help win the historic battle of Clavijo in which the Spaniards defeated the Moors.

As the Pilgrimage route to Jerusalem became more dangerous and slowly shut down because of the Crusades, the Way of St. James Way became increasingly popular for European monks and penitents. It rivaled and eventually surpassed the Pilgrimage to Rome as the best gateway to heaven. A vast support system grew up along the Pilgrims' way. Hospitals were built to provide shelter and healing. Orders of Knights, including the Knights Templar and the Order of Santiago, were formed to protect Pilgrims. Churches and cathedrals were built through the centuries. Kings and cultures fought over and defended territories.

You go over the Pyrenees to get to northern Spain. The passes between St. Jean Pied de Port in France and Roncesvalles in Spain were the ones used through the centuries by armies, invasions, migration, and Pilgrimage. This was historically and is still Basque country in both Spain and France.

The full name of the Pilgrimage is El Camino de Santiago de Compostela. Santiago is from Hebrew, Iago, to which Sant is prefixed. The word Compostela translates literally as field of stars. It is lost in the mist of time where the name came from. It possibly derives from the vision the soldier had of Sant Iago, or from the brightness of the Milky Way guiding Pilgrims, or possibly even from an ancient Roman cemetery in a field in Santiago de Compostela. Regardless, it is nice to know the whole name and spell it properly: El Camino de Santiago de Compostela. It is affectionately and often abbreviated to El Camino.

The route most walked is Camino Francés. It is the one hundreds of thousands of Pilgrims used during Medieval times and we walk now, and it is the route I walked. There are other routes: Portugal, Primitivo, and del Norte to name a few. There are also designated starting points in other towns and cities throughout Europe, creating a web of trails. Many Pilgrims throughout history, and some Pilgrims now, begin elsewhere. Unless they are in Spain or Portugal, there is the necessary passage over the Pyrenees. Thus most of the routes arrive at and continue on Camino Francés.

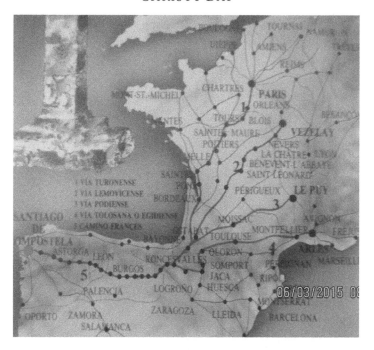

The more established the route became, the more protected it became – by kings, knights, soldiers, and now World Heritage. It is a beloved national treasure in Spain and is designated as such by the European Union as well, the Itinerario Cultural Europeo. You often ponder whose footsteps you walk in.

There was an outstanding write-up in a display in the museum in León as follows: "On the old Roman road, which had been a pre-historic path to the West, the legendary appearance of the tomb of St. James the Apostle revitalized the road that linked the finis terrae of Hispania to the lands beyond the Pyrenees. The route harmonized the Spanish kingdoms with Europe and helped populate the cities alongside it, strung like Rosary beads, with men, money, and skills, attracted by this land of opportunity and crusade, this Medieval 'far west' known as Jakobusland, the land of Santiago. It was a singular network of churches, inns and roads on which the images of the saint protected both Christian armies and the Pilgrims who streamed in from the farthest reaches of Christendom."

Chapter 2

PLANNING: DOWN TO THE NITTY GRITTY

If you really want to do something, you will find a way.
If you don't, you'll find an excuse.

~Author Unknown
(seen on a wall at Albergue Camino y Leyenda)

The traditional starting point for Camino Francés is on the French side of the Pyrenees in St. Jean Pied de Port. Some Pilgrims start in westernmost Spain in Roncesvalles which is what I did. Bus, train, plane and rental car can get you to either town.

Now is the time to check to see that your passport will be current for the time you are going.

It is vital to give a lot of thought to your equipment. You need a well-designed backpack, not too big and not too small. You should aim for your perfect pair of shoes matched to socks that are just right. Another important decision, mainly because of weather, is what season you want to walk. For the hard-core, winter sees extreme weather and lacks in support services. Summer can get extremely hot in northern Spain. Both spring and fall can have unpredictable weather (it's what ponchos and Gore-tex are for). There are inevitable challenges on El Camino, including weather, yet Pilgrims walk El Camino every day, and each Pilgrim chooses the timing to suit individual needs.

Plan ahead, pack ahead, and whatever season you choose, you will find other Pilgrims on the Way. Most of us from the far continents don't have the good fortune of being able to do it in stages like the Europeans do. Ours is all or nothing which adds to the challenge and the ultimate joy of success. If you can't do the entire route, figure out where you want to step on. Think about whether this will be your one El Camino experience or whether you want to do it in stages. Be prepared for that thought to change as you walk!

Start training. Walk, walk, walk, and walk some more before you go. Lose weight if you need to. Speak with your health care provider if there are health concerns (and even if there are not). Load up your backpack and walk with it. It will ensure an enjoyable time on the Pilgrimage and will make it more about the journey than about the pain. It is inevitably about the pain, too.

Respectfully learn enough Spanish before you go to order basic things, say please and thank you, and ask, in Spanish, "Do you speak English?" Good manners smooth the way to friendly communication and everyone I met was accommodating and helpful, be it ordering fresh squeezed orange juice or discussing a medical issue with a pharmacist. We figured it out working with a mix of both languages. Many Spaniards spoke impeccable English or they tolerated my beginner attempts at Spanish, and we mimed when necessary.

You are required to have your Pilgrim's Credencial and you need a guidebook. Go ahead and join your country's Pilgrim organization (for Americans, go to americanpilgrims.org). They are a wealth of information and if you are local, there is a local chapter where you can pick the brains of Pilgrims who have already walked. They also provide you with your Credencial.

Chapter 3

WHAT WE CARRY

To attain knowledge, add things every day.
To attain wisdom, remove things every day.

~Lao-tzu

This chapter is going to name brands and is meant to be neither endorsement nor advertising. Walking El Camino is an enormous undertaking and we can be in the dark about a lot of choices, some of them critical, that will affect our daily well-being. The right equipment makes the difference between completing the Pilgrimage and being stopped in our tracks. It would have helped me to know brands and products that worked for another Pilgrim. Having said that, it is important to remember that this will be your Pilgrimage and you must inevitably come to your own best decisions. Be mindful of the fact that whatever choices you make, you will be hauling them on your back or dealing with them every step of the Way.

As to equipment, particularly your shoes, socks, and backpack, do as much research as you can. Talk with walkers, hikers, backpackers, and Pilgrims if you can. Utilize the expertise of your favorite hiking, camping & sporting goods stores. Pick the brains of experts you know. Ask yourself: Do I need it or is it a what-if? Does it sustain my long journey? Is it the lightest weight it can possibly be? Balance the weight of what you think you need with how vital it is to your Pilgrimage.

Bring a journal, a pen or two, and a little camera. Hat and dark glasses are a must. Sunscreen is an absolute must. I applied it religiously to my face two or three times a day. I wouldn't have survived without my wide-brimmed hat for both sun and rain. Bring something toasty and long sleeve. Wear short sleeves mostly. Zip-off pants are an excellent choice. Quick-drying clothes make daily laundry a breeze. Be practical. You don't have to have everything new and state of the art. Challenge yourself to use what you already own when you can.

The guidebook you need is John Brierley's *A Pilgrim's Guide to the Camino de Santiago, St. Jean-Roncesvalles-Santiago: A Practical & Mystical Manual for the Modern Day Pilgrim*. It is updated every year and I saw copies from many years and in many languages. He publishes the go-to guide book for the other 12 routes as well. You can order it through your local bookstore or on-line. It is lightweight and the only book you need in your backpack. Brierley divides the route into suggested reasonable stages and he gives you information about the daily walking and the support services along the Way. There's a nice mixture of reflections, quotes, and meditations. Churches, cathedrals, particular points of interest, as well as not-to-be-missed works of art, statuary, and sights along the Way are discussed. He offers the deep surround of history. He has daily meditations and inspiring quotes. There is a comprehensive list of suggested items to bring.

The Credencial del Peregrino is required. This is the Pilgrim's Passport. You cannot step foot in the albergues without this credencial. You are obligated to have it stamped every day where you stay and you can also get it stamped at restaurants and business establishments. It ultimately becomes a beautiful little memento of your time on El Camino. At the Pilgrim Office in Santiago de Compostela, it is carefully inspected, dates are verified, and then they add their stamp to it and give you your gorgeous Compastela Certificate, written in 14th century Latin.

As stated previously, in the US you can request this Credencial del Peregrino/Pilgrim's Passport from americanpilgrims.org. If your first one gets filled with the required stamps, you can obtain a second one on The Way. Be sure to get it two months before you plan to go. This would be a good time to also make sure your real passport hasn't expired!

I am starting with the shoes because your feet are the foundation of your Pilgrimage. There are many opinions about footwear and ultimately you will have to decide. Though El Camino is not wilderness trekking, it is also not a walk in the park. There is plenty of steep terrain and the walking surface is often rough, rocky, or uneven. Sometimes it is slippery and muddy. Your feet take a real pounding. Oh! How I grew to dislike a cobblestone surface. Multiply this over hundreds of miles and it matters that you are well-supported from the ground up. You want shoes with sturdy, gripping soles. Your first choice is between walking shoes and walking boots. Heavy duty hiking boots aren't necessary, in my humble opinion, and I saw plenty of boots hanging off backpacks and in donation boxes (as opposed to on feet).

After lengthy conversations with the shoe experts at my favorite outdoor store, I decided on walking shoes not boots. I tried on pairs in my size and in a half size and full size larger to make room for mild swelling and for comfort. You want them comfy and roomy yet snug enough to support. You invite blisters by having shoes that are either too roomy or too tight. I tried on at least a dozen pair in three sizes and when I tried on a Salomon a half size larger than my usual size, bingo! They were the Goldilocks "just right" pair of shoes. They had the sturdiness, the comfort, the fit. They were Gore-tex so they breathed and were water-proof. They were comfortable as all get-out. I heard and read more than once of Pilgrims being advised to buy shoes two sizes bigger than their regular size. I implore you, don't! It is a recipe for disaster because you not only don't get the support you need, you also are more likely to get blisters from your feet moving around too much in your shoes.

Break them in before you go!

Next came socks. Again, consult with experts and friends. You will get as many opinions as there are people and will have to decide. Smart

Wool and Vermont's Darned Tough were the ones for me. They are both made of merino wool. I chose two styles, one much thicker overall and one which felt like it was super-padded underneath. Both pairs were hiking socks. I brought along two pairs of each because I didn't know which would work best. I tried both with my shoes in advance to make sure they were comfortable. Wool wicked the sweat outward to the Gore-Tex. The cushy feeling underfoot seems to have protected my feet from damage and sore heels. It was nice to have two different thicknesses to work with, depending on how tender and swollen my feet were on any given day.

Cotton socks are the least recommended because they don't wick sweat. I've often wondered if my feet would have done better with a light wicking liner sock underneath the wool socks.

You need a second pair of shoes to change into at the end of each day of walking. Some people bring easily replaceable flip-flops. I chose to bring a pair of North Face, lightweight sandals with Velcro straps and open toes. They proved to be sturdy and comfortable enough to walk around the cities and towns for sightseeing and go to dinner in. My toes liked being open to the air. They were knock-about enough to wear into the showers and around the Albergues.

After much searching, researching, and investigating in person and on-line, I ended up getting a North Face Terra 50 backpack, 50-liter capacity. I might have gotten away with a Terra 40. Do not -do not, do not, do not - get a big backpack. You will inevitably be tempted to fill it with "what ifs" that you think you might need. If you lug extraneous weight around, your feet, your joints, your back, and your brain will pay for your regrettable choices. The pack's design worked well for me. It clipped tightly shut, had a zippered cover, roomy main compartment, and a separate bottom sleeping bag compartment. There were nice small compartments on the belt as well, a couple of good pockets, some other zippered areas, and well-designed walking stick holders. I liked that it gave me options for easy access to oft-used gear, and it was designed to balance the load well on my hips. It also had fine-tuning adjustment straps that made all the difference when it came to carrying the weight optimally.

It's important to get all the straps adjusted so that your hips carry the weight. Friends, family, hiking store expert can help with this. It is also smart to get in the habit of hoisting the pack gently to your back, bracing it on a bent knee first, as opposed to wresting it up. You potentially save pulled muscles.

I brought an old rain poncho. It kept me dry and simultaneously served well as rain cover for my back pack. It came completely apart and I replaced it cheaply with another one halfway through the Pilgrimage. A rain coat is just as good a choice, in which case you need a back pack cover. My lightweight windbreaker protected adequately in most conditions. I saw a lot of Gore-Tex as well as inexpensive rain suits, and nice rain pack covers, too. Replacements are readily available along The Way.

You need at most a lightweight sleeping bag. Mine weighed two pounds and I could have tweaked that down. Some Pilgrims just bring a sleeping sheet. Most Albergues provide blankets that you can use in lieu of or in combination with your own gear.

Walking poles (or not) are entirely a matter of personal choice. Lots of people buy a wooden walking staff en route which often comes with a gourd and scallop shell attached, which are the traditional symbols of El Camino. I opted for lightweight aluminum poles. I was particularly grateful for them in the first days of walking when they took pressure off my joints and, despite my training, my relatively unconditioned muscles, especially going downhill and on rocky trails. There is evidence that they relieve a statistically significant burden from your joints. They stabilized me on a couple of windy days on rocky terrain.

In the river rafting and hiking communities, Dr. Bronner's liquid soap is an old standby. It's gentle on the environment and tough on dirt and odors. An excellent cleaner, it comes in pleasant natural scents (I chose lavender), and a little bit goes a long way. To comply with TSA, I filled a 3 oz. container with it and it was more than sufficient for the entire Pilgrimage. It was my all-purpose liquid soap for face, hair, body, laundry, and dishes.

I wanted a lightweight towel and a Shamwow! did the trick. Now is not the time for a luxury bath sheet. I liked that it absorbed a lot of water efficiently, dried quickly, and that it was small and light in my pack. Hiking stores have a nice variety of microfiber towels in various sizes. You'd be amazed at how small it can be and still dry you off completely. I used large safety pins (imperdibles in Spanish – "unlosables") to hang wet clothes on clothes-lines and on my back pack.

You know what you need to bring in terms of meds. Consult Brierley's book for a comprehensive list. I didn't bring painkillers or antihistamines. I did bring antibiotic ointment. Stopping an infection before it becomes a hospital issue is critical. I brought nasal strips to prevent me snoring. As it turned out, it was a fine chorus of snorers I joined so I didn't have to use them. I did use them on one long uphill day to give me more oxygen. The difference was noticeable.

I met a couple from the U.S. who sent home a shocking 15 pounds of what-ifs. What were my what-ifs, the ones that I shipped home part way through the Pilgrimage? They included my little water filter (reliable, potable water was never an issue), inflatable sleeping pad (always had a bunk to sleep in), earmuffs, gloves, camping plate, mug, spoon, and fork. Three and a half pounds doesn't sound like much, really, yet my pack felt significantly lighter and my body and spirit were buoyed by the change.

It is possible, as John Brierley states in his guide book, to walk El Camino on $25-30 a day. Bring quite a lot of cash because there aren't ATM's in every town and many places don't take credit or debit cards. The municipal albergues and most other albergues cost $5-15 a night. Pilgrims' menu – filling and usually downright delicious – is $8-10 a night. Snacks, breakfast, lunch, coffee, treats and more treats amount to $5-10 a day. One or two rest days to reconfigure yourself, see museums, soak in a real bathtub, don't add much to your budget. I walked for 39 days with two days' rest. Many Pilgrims do it in 33 days. The shorter the time, obviously, the less you spend.

Finally, know this: You are not heading into unsupported wilderness.

Spaniards have been tending to Pilgrims for over 1200 years. There are pharmacies, grocery stores, tiendas, sporting goods stores, shoe stores and tourist shops in most towns and cities along El Camino. Many of them cater to the specific needs of Pilgrims. What you forgot, what you need to replenish, and what you decide you need, you can easily find. I regretted not having a bottle of lavender essential oil and was thrilled to find it at a little Monastery store. When my bedraggled old poncho ripped apart, I got an inexpensive replacement in a "Bazaar," the Spanish version of our Dollar Stores.

All things feet are covered in the next chapter.

Chapter 4

FEET: THE SOUL OF THE JOURNEY

*It is possible to fail in many ways…while to succeed
is possible in only one way.*

~Aristotle

Day One walking is when you begin to find out whether you made the right choices for your feet. The first afternoon, people start to treat injuries and start practicing their protocol. Here is what happened to my feet. Here's what worked. Brace yourself for brand names once again.

Foot injuries, foot pain, and foot infections are probably the biggest health issue on El Camino. Some of it is generated by lack of conditioning, some from having the wrong footwear, and some of it is from not tending to your feet. It is also caused by overdoing it early on, demanding too much of your body, and part of it is caused by not zealously paying attention to what is going on. We all learned as we walked. Amazingly, despite a lot of pain, most Pilgrims finish the walk. Decide that you will too.

I never did experience extreme tenderness, muscle strain, injured heels, plantar fasciitis, Achilles heel, severe infections, sprained ankle, or bone breaks. I saw plenty of them. I got quite a few small blisters and a huge one on one of my big toes. None of them required me to stop for an extra day. A German woman generously gave me some of her Compeed (sold in the US as a Band-Aid product). What a miracle bandage that is. Compeed draws the water out of the blister, seals the blister off, and then in hydro-colloidal action, uses the water as padding to protect the blister. When it has done its job, when the blister has healed and new skin has formed, it comes off all by itself, usually in four or five days. You are cautioned not to tear the bandage off as you risk tearing off newly formed skin as well.

I used up most of a tube of antibiotic ointment – it seemed like cheap insurance and my mild infections went away usually overnight. I did not apply Compeed until any area was definitely free of infection because it would lock the infection in.

I also made generous use of 1½ inch medical tape to protect hot spots before they became blisters and for the days that blisters were callousing over. I also used liquid bandage to protect tender and potentially abraded areas. I preferred both of these products to Band-Aids because they stayed in place better.

As the weeks passed, I had to use fewer and fewer products in fewer and fewer places. What you use for foot care is another area that you want to consult with experts and friends and then make your own best decision. You will get plenty of advice and support on The Way! I wish I had had Compeed from the get-go. In retrospect, the wide medical tape was one of the most important items in my kit. In fact, I had to buy a replacement roll at a pharmacy on the Way. My feet would not have surived without these two items.

Every day, just as soon as I had claimed my bunk, I tended to my feet. I removed my socks, bathed my feet and then applied moisturizer with 4 drops of lavender mixed in. I gave my feet a good massage and then did Jin Shin Jiyistu, a Japanese energy point touch therapy. After that I assessed present and potential damage and trouble. If callouses needed filing, I did so, and I trimmed my toenails as well. If Compeed was ready to come off, I removed it. I inspected each piece of tape and decided whether to remove it or leave it for another day. Lavender helps with infections and its scent is soothing. I applied antibiotic ointment then and at bedtime. I replaced bandages, removed them, inspected for infection, let my feet air out. By the time I put on my open toe sandals my feet were good to go.

Theories abound in the healthy feet department, and I think many of us, including myself, thought that it would just work itself out. In most cases it did. Others started the walk with tried and true methods that kept their feet fit and happy. Others, I suspect, also started the Way in better physical condition than I which stressed their feet less. Following is some of what I learned along the Way. Fellow Pilgrims generously shared their ideas, knowledge, and the products in their Healthy Feet Kit. The second day, I gave my container of Vaseline to a bunkmate and when we saw each other weeks later, he told me what a lifesaver it had been.

Some people swore by massaging Vaseline into their feet when they arrived and in the morning before setting out. Others took off their shoes and socks during the daily walk, once, twice, even every hour. Some Pilgrims used duct tape instead of medical tape. At several albergues, I soaked my feet in warm salt water with a splash of vinegar. There was a variety of socks – wool like mine, doubled up pairs with a thin inner sock for wicking, hi-tech socks. You and your hiking store – and your budget - will figure out what is best. Shoes and socks are truly the one place you should go for the best.

One of the things that affected my feet was an overall lack of conditioning in general. My muscles didn't adequately support my feet and joints and everything just plain hurt at the end of the day from the feet up. As the Way wore on, I felt better and better and so did my feet.

Pay attention and start treating issues as you know they are developing, even if it's mid-walk, mid-day. I never did figure out why I got the blisters I did. Though they weren't debilitating, they were aggravating. Despite training, I think my feet weren't toughened up. Steep downhills crammed my toes into the front of my shoes. Even though I thought I did, perhaps I didn't have my toenails closely enough clipped at the beginning. I didn't take my shoes off during the morning walk and let my feet air out. I didn't start moisturizing my feet on Day 1. I didn't add lavender essential oil to the moisturizer until well into the Pilgrimage.

I have mildly deformed feet to begin with - small bunions, corns, and a bent-up toe that was broken in childhood. Cram those into shoes and they just beg for blisters. I lost my right big toenail on Day 19 and I nearly fainted I was so shocked. Though I feared it might be a deal breaker, it wasn't. All I needed to do was wrap my toe in medical tape and there was no pain. Photos I took of my feet en route confirm that they went from looking like walking disasters to minimally damaged in six weeks' time.

Spoiler alert: Gross photos of feet.

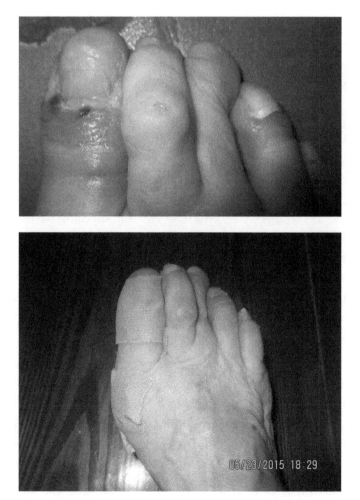

Chapter 5

MUNI MANNERS (AND MADNESS)

We find our path by walking it.
~Maya Angelou.

Municipal albergues house the many. Sometimes you are in a bunkroom with fifty or a hundred people, sometimes just a few (and on rare occasions, just yourself). Lights, formally or casually, go out around 10 p.m. and come on in the morning never before 6:00. At some moment between 5:15 and 5:30, you hear the first zzzzt of a sleeping bag zipper and the hive comes alive. Soon the noises of making ready for the day surround you. Here are some common sense rules to help others keep their sanity in this quiet mayhem.

Do lay out your clothes and pack your pack the night before. Do honor people going to bed early by being quiet. Do plan your departure for maximum efficiency and least amount of noise. It was fun to see just how efficient I could be and it got so I could be dressed and out of the bunk room in the dark in five minutes without disturbing a soul. I liked taking off just before dawn so I could catch the coolness of the morning and watch the sunrise over a city or in the countryside.

You are expected to claim a space for yourself near the bunk and everyone will honor it. Don't take up more than your fair share. Pay attention to whether a particular Albergue wants doors shut, lights put on. Follow the written rules. Don't slam the doors. Honor the lights out/quiet down time. This is all so common-sensical it's ridiculous and it is equally ridiculous how often Pilgrims blithely ignored it.

Don't assume because you are awake and eager to set off that everyone around you feels the same way. Please don't set your cell phone alarm for before 6 a.m. Don't check your cell phone for a.m. messages. Don't take cell phone calls in the bunk room, day or night. Don't shine your flashlight or cell phone into other people's eyes (seriously, I have to say that?). At dawn's break it is thoughtful not to rustle to the bottom of your pack, through foil and paper and bags, to get at something and then reverse the procedure.

Chapter 6

DAY BY DAY

If we are facing in the right direction, all we have to do is keep on walking.

~Buddha

DAY 1, *April 22.*   Roncesvalles to Zubiri. 21 km/12.6 miles. Albergue Rio Arga Ibaia.

DAY 2, *April 23.*   Zubiri to Pamplona. 22.2 km/13.2 miles. Albergue Jésus y Maria.

DAY 3, *April 24.*   Pamplona to Obanós. 24.2 km/13.6 miles. Albergue USDA. Passed monument peregrine.

DAY 4, *April 25.*   Obanós to Villatuerta. 20.8 km/12.5 miles. Casa Magica.

DAY 5, *April 26.*   Villatuerta to Villa Mayor de Monjardín. V de M Albegue. 11.9 km/7.2 miles. Irache free wine fountain in Estella. a.m. cup of vino tinto.

DAY 6, *April 27.*   Villa Mayor de Monjardín to Torres del Rio. Albergue Casa Mariela.

DAY 7, *April 28.*   Torres del Rio to Logróno. 20.6 km/12.3 miles. Albergue Santiago Apostal. Rioja Country!

DAY 8, *April 29.*   Logroño to Ventosa. 18.8 km/11.5 miles. Albergue San Saturnino.

DAY 9, *April 30.*   Ventosa to Azofra. 16 km/9.6 miles. Albergue Municipal de Peregrinos w/fountain/pool/courtyard.

DAY 10, *May 1.*   Azofra to Grañón. 21.1 km/12.6 miles. St. John The Baptist, donativo, cooked together. 15 yoga mats.

DAY 11, *May 2.*   Grañón to Belorado. 15.4 km/9.7 miles. Albergue-Restaurante a Santiago Belorado. Email!

DAY 12, *May 3.*   Belorado to San Juan de Ortega. 24.3 km/15.1 miles.Santaurio San Juan de Orgega. Civil War monument. Bunk mate Jerry from Ireland w/ story of his boss who fought in Lincoln US International Brigade. Held for 2 years in Burgos Prison which Jerry visits tomorrow.

DAY 13, *May 4.*   San Juan de Ortega to Burgos. 26.4 km/16.4 miles. 600 bed Amigos del Camino de Santiago Burgos. Saw Kenth.

DAY 14, *May 5.*   Burgos Day of rest. El Cid Hotel 65 Euros. Toured cathedral, 2nd largest in Spain.

DAY 15, *May 6.* Burgos to Hornillos delCamino. 21 km/13.0 Miles. Albergue Municipal. Yummy beef stew On the meseta.

DAY 16, *May 7.* Hornillos del Camino to Castrojeriz. 20.2 km/12.6 miles. 20.2 km/12.1 miles. Albergue Casa Nosra -500-year-old house, Castle ruins on top of hill, San Anton Convent ruins.

DAY 17, *May 8.* Castrojeriz to Boadilla del Camino. 20 km/12 Miles. Stayed muni 5 Euros but lots of time in most amazing albergue courtyard food computer love and gorgeous painting over fabulous dinner.

DAY 18, *May 9.* Boadilla del Camino to Villalcázar de Sirga. 20.5km/12.3 miles. Muni Albergue. Walked through flock of sheep. Fabulous Knights Templar Church w/ rose window.

DAY 19, *May 10.* Villalcázar de Sirga to Caldadilla de la Cueza. 21.7 km/13 miles. Incredible lamb dinner.

DAY 20, *May 11.* Caldadilla de la Cueza to Sahagún. 21.7 km/13 miles. Albergue Municipal w/ cubicles. Cooked with Ryan from Montreal.

DAY 21, *May 12.* Sahagún to Calzada de los Hermanillos.

13.9 km/8.3 miles. Alone all day on Roman Way. Hungarian bunkmates Tomas (16) and Chubba. Chris and Angela from England were there. Money bus. Albergue Muni.

DAY 22, *May 13.* Calzada de los Hermanillos to Mansilla de las Mulas. 24.5 km/15.2 miles. Amigos del Peregrino Albergue.

DAY 23, *May 14.* Mansilla de las Mulas to León. 18.1 km/11.2

miles. Benedictinas Santa Maria de Carbajal Albergue. Mailed 3½ pound box home. Blessing by the Nuns. Sister Monica. Lost Susan's bracelet.

DAY 24, *May 15.*   Day of rest, León. Albany Hotel sold me 45 Euro room in apt bldg. Museum. Forgot to have my credencial stamped.

DAY 25, *May 16.*   León to Villar de Mazarife. 21.8 km/13.5 miles. Refugio de Jésus. Got really sick. Bunked w/ Natasha & Francal, South Africa.

DAY 26, *May 17.*   Villar de Mazarife to Hospital de Orbigo. 14.4 km/8.6 miles. Real struggle, practically crawled there. Found Sangha Amezen Albergue (Buddhist sanctuary) with pictures of Thich Nhat Han and chanting to heal by. Stepa my only housemate, Croatian, also León food poisoning.

DAY 27, *May 18.*   Hospital de Orbigo to Astorga.16.8 km/10.8 miles. Gaudí Bishop's Palace. Saw Stepa. Albergue Amigos del Camino de Santiago Astorga.

DAY 28, *May 19.*   Astorga to Rabanal del Camino. 20.6 km/12.8 miles. Passed by Cowboy Bar. Albergue el Pilar. Evening blessing – sat up front w/ soprano.

DAY 29, *May 20.*   Rabanal del Camino to Acebo. 16.7 km/10 miles. 32ºF today. Wore every piece of clothing. Forgot to leave stone & message at cross. Highest point on the Way today, almost 5,000'. Albergue Meson el Acerbo. Stone hillside houses. Ate w/ Austin, the British architect who does incredible pen and ink renderings. He also introduced me to Magno, the delightful Spanish brandy.

DAY 30, *May 21.* Acebo to Ponferrada. 18.2 km/10.9 miles. Albergue San Nicolás de Flüe (Swiss). Awesome 12th c. Knights Templar Castle. Bought wine at Gas station & cooked dinner entirely of free food in fridge & on shelves.

DAY 31, *May 22.* Ponferrada to Cacabelos. 17.6 km/10.7 miles. Albergue Municipal in Church Capilla de las Angustia. Two beds/room, w/ German woman. Walked across bridge for delightful seafood paella dinner.

DAY 32, *May 23.* Cacabelos to Trabadelo. 20.2 km/12.1 Miles. Got seriously lost in Villafranca del Bierzo. Followed old highway. Saw Doroty at fabuloso Albergue Camino y Leyenda – own room w/ real twin bed, real sheets, balcony. A library – read a great book about El Camino. What a shower.

DAY 33, *May 24.* Trabadelo to O Cebreiro. 18.7 km/11.2 miles. 5 miles continuous uphill. I did it! Horses from bottom to top for some. Bagpipe music in Laguna de Castilla. BB King is dead. Municipal Albergue Xunta. 9th c. church – oldest on El Camino.

DAY 34, *May 25.* O'Cebreiro to Triacastela. 20.7 km/12.9 miles. Foggy start up top. Shaded much of way. Albergue de Triacastela way down in field with Treacherous non-path to clothes lines. Fabulous Dinner of lentils and lamb, me the only Pilgrim. Crazy Spanish guy sleep walked into our room in middle of night.

DAY 35, *May 26.*   Triacastela to Sarria. 18.7 km/12.6 miles. Chose not to go to Samos. Austin did. One of largest monasteries in world & it has only 11 monks. Brand new Oasis Albergue.

DAY 36, *May 27.*   Sarria to Portomarín. 22.1 km/13.7 miles. 100 steep steps after long bridge. Last lower Bunk @ Albergue Ultreia. Ate w/ Austin.

DAY 37, *May 28.*   Portomarín to Portos. 19.2 km/11.5 miles. A Paso Formigo w/ ant sculptures. Paella. Membrillo. Gazpacho. German man w/ 8 year old son checked in. Austin showed up and we parted as I set out for Vilar de Donas-Igrexa San Salvador. Knights of Santiago buried here. Originally 9th c. nunnery. After dinner drink & heartwarming conversation w/ Georg.

DAY 38, *May 29.*   Portos to Melide. 20.2 km/12.1 miles. Albergue O Cruceiro.

DAY 39, *May 30.*   Almost there! Melide to Arzúa. 15 km/9 Miles. Albergue da Fonte. Mandala Restaurant. Afternoon, cocoa w/ Giuliano (Brazilian lives in Miami Beach). Plaza party then Queimada blessing ceremony. Albergue w/ French tourists, rolling luggage that'd hold 3 backpacks.

DAY 40, *May 31.*   Arzúa to O Pedrouzo. 19.2 km/11.5 miles. Highway into town. T-shirt for Julia. Walked w/Hospitalero who knew Swiss Mike at Flüe Alb.

DAY 41. *June 1.*   19.8 km/12.3 miles. Oh my gosh, today's the day after 39 days of walking! Asked a fellow Pilgrim how to fully prostrate. Ran into Doroty on the way into Santiago de Compostela. Came close to badly hurt by a cyclist. Arrived at Cathedral at 12:30. Had a San Francisco tourist take my photo fully prostrated. Other tourists then took my photo. Nest Style Hotel. Real hotel, real room.

DAY 42, *June 2.*   Pilgrims Mass. Saw the Botafumeiro fly!

DAY 43, *June 3.*   Shopped. Lamb dinner. Bumped into Georg and also Jennifer from León.

Chapter 7

THE WORLD WALKS EL CAMINO

If we have no peace it is because we have forgotten,
we belong to each other.

~Mother Teresa

The night before I left, my daughter, Julia, and I attended the Pilgrims' Mass and a Blessing by the priests. They said the blessing in seven languages, including Korean, based on the Pilgrims they knew to be checked in that night. One of the priests said that although this used to be a Catholic Pilgrimage, it is now a Pilgrimage for the whole world. He reminded us that we are all children of God, and he encouraged us to walk in peace on El Camino. He encouraged us to take care of each other, and he said that if I saw someone in need, I should help them. Likewise, fellow Pilgrims would no doubt be there to help me if I needed it. How true that turned out to be! He prayed for us to bring that peace back to the world.

This is what Julia wrote in my journal about what the priests said, "On the Way, try and spread peace and friendship to all whom you encounter. In the way of life, take the lessons of El Camino and make the world a better, happier, more peaceful place, full of love and friendships. You will meet people from all over the world, from many walks of life. Do not turn them away."

I walked with at least 40 countries. I say at least because these are the ones I know from asking. I didn't start finding out where people were from until several days in. Sometimes a language barrier made it impossible to find out where someone was from.

Alphabetically, the countries were:

Argentina	Germany	Scotland
Australia	Hungary	Slovakia
Austria	Ireland	Slovenia
Brazil	Israel	South Africa
Bulgaria	Italy	South Korea
Canada *(all ten provinces)*	Japan	Spain
China	Mexico	Sweden
Columbia	Nepal	Switzerland
Croatia	New Zealand	The Netherlands
Czech Republic	Norway	United States *(from at least 17 states)*
Denmark	Paraguay	Uruguay
England	Poland	Venezuela
France	Portugal	Wales
	Romania	

The youngest Pilgrim I met was 8, a German kid walking the last 100 kilometers with his dad. The oldest I met was 78.

Cirauqui

Torres del Río Church of the Holy Sepulchre

Burgos

St. James

Oldest cross on El Camino

Castrojeriz

Hornillos del Camino

On the Meseta

Gaudí's Bishop's Palace, Astorga

Sahagún, Ermita Virgen del Puente

On the high Meseta

Mooooo!

Cruz de Ferro. Add your stone to the pile.

Especially nice El Camino Marker

Long climb to O'Cebreiro

O'Cebreiro. Celtic stone house with thatched roof.

Hospital di Orbigo. Longest Roman bridge on El Camino.

El Bierzo vineyard

Castillo de los Templarios, Ponferrada.

Mountain in the fog west of O'Cebreiro.

Villalcázar de Sirga, Templar church of Santa María la Virgen Blanca.

Route Signage.

Burgos. Second largest cathedral in Spain.

*Stone Church in O'Cebreiro. Oldest
church on the Way.*

Cathedral in León.

Cathedral in Santiago de Compostela

*Botafumeiro, giant incense burner
in the Cathedral.*

Everyone – everyone – on El Camino de Santiago de Compostela understood "Buen Camino" and everyone greeted Pilgrims with it.

The Pilgrims Office in Santiago de Compostela keeps statistics on who receives their Compostela and they publish them annually. The stats are broken down by gender, whether on foot, by bike, on horseback, or wheelchair; by age, top nationalities, which Camino was walked and the starting point for each Pilgrim. You can start walking anywhere along the Pilgrimage and to collect your Compostela you have to have walked a minimum of the last hundred kilometers (62 miles). These stats are fun to read after the fact because they give you an objective glimpse, a snapshot if you will, of who is on the Pilgrimage and the individual grit and determination it takes. In a way, it is a self-congratulatory pat on the back for having stuck it out. I didn't know the statistics existed until I returned home and I was amazed at my cohort group. It made me even more pleased that I had decided from the get-go to walk every inch of the way under my own steam and to carry my backpack every inch of the way.

I am a 66 years old female from the United States who walked Camino Francés in 2015. In 2013, of the 215,880 Pilgrims who received their Compostela, 70% walked El Camino Francés. 45% were women and 87% completed it on foot. 15% were 60 or older. 9% were from the United States. 12% started on the French side of the Pyrenees and a mere 3% started in Roncesvalles (the sign in Roncesvalles said 790 km to Santiago).

Chapter 8

PRACTICAL ADVICE FOR
KEEPING YOURSELF SAFE

It is important to trust your gut and to keep yourself out of harm's way. If something doesn't feel right, attach yourself to fellow Pilgrims (who will always welcome you gladly). If the streets feel lonely or dark, wait for fellow walkers and join them. Though I never felt any particular danger on El Camino, I did exercise caution. In the big cities, I made sure I was in by dark or that I walked with fellow Pilgrims. Don't be afraid to ask if you can walk together. A middle aged American woman disappeared in April, 2015. Her name is Denise Thiem, she was 41, from Arizona. At the time I was walking, she was missing and I saw posters asking for help finding her. At several of the Pilgrim Blessings, we were asked to keep her in our prayers. Her body was found after I returned home and she had been murdered.

Don't assume because you are a Pilgrim that you are safe. You are not. In some ways I suppose you might even be a bit of a target. So even though I felt safe, I took numerous precautions with myself and my belongings. It worked for me, for example, to never, ever remove my purse from my body. The way I wore it was doubly secure because backpack waist strap cinched through it.

When I was walking around after I checked into the albergue for the day, I always wore my little purse across my shoulder. Along the way, I usually felt comfortable leaving my pack outside whenever I stopped, but certainly not my purse. Again, I trusted my gut, and if I felt at all worried, I took it off and leaned it against the wall inside. There is a protocol for this as you go along and you will quickly figure out how to stash it safely and at the same time keep it out of the way of fellow Pilgrims. I think my experience is typical – that you need not worry for a second about fellow Pilgrims pilfering your bag. It's even more important, of course, to keep yourself safe, which is really using common sense, as it is anywhere.

Chapter 9

HOME AWAY FROM HOME

Keep walking though there's no place to get to.
Don't try to see through the distances

~sign in Hornillos

When I got Brierley's guidebook, I immediately wanted to start mapping out my Pilgrimage. I couldn't figure out why I couldn't dig into that challenge before I left. I finally resigned myself to that fact that I wasn't going to and it wasn't until I got on El Camino that I realized it's impossible to do in advance. Every day is built around where you stayed the night before. Even if you follow his book exactly, breaking the Pilgrimage into 33 stages, you still can't plan ahead because there are so many options at each stop, and you might not make it as far as you had hoped. The lesson for me was to let go of this worry and to relax into the moment of every day. It is challenging and then you start to get a rhythm going. As you get a feel for what your body and soul will allow, you get a feel for what you will do the next day. You will get in the habit of planning the next day's walk and then you will improvise. I wish I had done this from the start. The journey unfolds exactly as it is supposed to.

Every day you get better and better at figuring out how to interpret and utilize the book for your Pilgrimage. Fellow Pilgrims will be offering their ideas. Your feet and body will let you know when to stop. Pretty soon, you are into a comfortable routine of reading and deciding. You will wonder what your angst was about.

The Pilgrim hostels are called albergues. There are six different kinds, and you will probably sample them all and start finding your preference. Sometimes I was guided by Brierley. Other times, I was exhausted and checked into the first albergue I came to. Often, I'd be walking with a fellow Pilgrim and they would tell me where they were planning to stay that night or suggest a place. You get to experience everything from Medieval to ultra-modern and everything in between. Almost without exception, you will be treated graciously, warmly, and hospitably. Brierley's book distinguishes them by type on his maps. There are municipals, run by the town. Convents and Monasteries are run respectively by nuns and priests. Parish hostels are owned by the diocese. There's a small group of private albergues that have formed a loose association to insure high quality. Finally, there are private albergues whose prices and services vary. You will find all you need on this in Brierley and you don't have to concern yourself with figuring it out before you go. It amazes me in retrospect to look back on some of my favorites and realize that I tumbled to them – either following a friend, or checking them out as I was walking by, or by dragging myself in by my sore bootstraps.

You are made welcome in all of them.

The food was fabulous – sometimes simple, sometimes gourmet, always, it seemed, lovingly made. Though you can eat a la carte everywhere, I highly recommend the Pilgrims' Menu, offered in most towns. It consisted of four or five courses, several choices in each course, red wine, water, bread, dessert. The Santiago almond cake is divine. It was easy and ample and you have the opportunity to mingle with other Pilgrims. I had several lamb dishes and a lentil soup that I will never forget. There are regional specialties offered on the Pilgrims' Menu. Try them! While I am on the subject of food, several years ago I found a treasure of a book and when I came home I was delighted to find that it had recipes for some of the traditional foods served on the Way, including Spanish tortilla, empanada, and Santiago almond cake. Though they are not the easiest to make, I succeeded in cooking them up to serve to friends when they came to hear about the Pilgrimage. The book is *Classic Spanish Cooking* by Elizabeth Luard.

If you really want to indulge yourself, occasionally or for the entire Way, there are first class hotels and inns and you can make reservations on your cell phone. I chose not to do this because I wanted the experience of trusting that El Camino would take care of me. I truly did and it truly did. I took Brierley's advice and had a day and night of rest in Burgos and in León. People at home wondered why I stayed only one extra night and it's because The Way enchants you and you want to be back in the flow. You get restless and want to be walking again and to see how the rest of your Pilgrimage is going to unfold. You feel like you're being left behind.

Chapter 10

A REALLY BRIEF HISTORY OF SPAIN

*"We find after years of struggle that we do not take a trip.
A trip takes us."*

~John Steinbeck.

El Camino de Santiago de Compostela is saturated in history, legend, story, and the footsteps of those who walked before us. You often ponder whose footsteps you walk in. You pass through much that is Neolithic, pre-history, Bronze Age. The Romans started making it part of their Empire around 19 A.D. An advanced Moslem community asserted itself on the Iberian Peninsula in 711. According to a write-up I saw in the museum in León, the Pilgrim's Route was the most "fluid connection" to the rest of Europe. The Pilgrimage began in the late 800's, possibly 885 A.D. Christian military campaigns began in 1085. You are literally walking through layers of history.

You walk through a complicated history as you walk across northern Spain. You pass through eleven provinces and three autonomous regions. Though it is impossible, of course, to absorb it all, it is fun to put pieces of the puzzle together. Take the time to appreciate the magnificent art, the glorious artifacts, fabulous statuary, and religious relics you will encounter. There are dazzling cathedrals and precious little chapels. You have the opportunity to see immense castles and ruins of castles and monasteries. Treasures abound in every church and in the tiniest towns. The cities have world-famous museums. Brierley's guidebook is replete with information. Don't be dismayed that you won't see it all. You simply can't. Everything you do absorb will be part of your Pilgrim story, and you will be fascinated as you create your own mythology of The Way.

"The Song of Roland" is the epic poem about Charlemagne's nephew and the Battle of Roncesvaux (Roncesvalles) of 778. It was written sometime between 1040 and 1115. Roland was killed in this battle. The huge albergue in Roncesvalles was built by Charlemagne – imagine that!

The Museum in León does a fabulous job of explaining Spain's rich and complex history. All the cathedrals and churches are repositories of the story. The cathedral in Burgos has the most artifacts and even the tiniest towns have priceless treasures.

The Knights Templar Castle in Ponferrada had interesting information on castles in general. It is one of the best-preserved castles in Europe (that isn't lived in). Until castles were made obsolete by gunpowder in the 16th century, they were the equivalent of modern day nuclear weapons. They were pretty much impregnable and campaigns against castles were costly and often not successful. Few castles were captured. Society was structured around Church and Clergy, Knights, Peasants, and the Aristocracy, and castles were the stronghold.

James Michener's delightful book, *Iberia,* has an outstanding chapter on El Camino, the history, myth, and lore. "It is difficult to describe, in a scientific age, the spiritual hold that Pilgrimage had on citizens of the Middle Ages. There was, of course, in those days, but one Church, and so far as the Christian world was concerned, it was truly universal. Existence outside the membership of this religion was unthinkable, and the three physical locations upon which the imagery of the Church depended were Jerusalem, where Christ was crucified; Rome, where Peter founded the organization of the Church; and Compostela, from which point Europe had been evangelized. Any Christian who made a Pilgrimage to one of these places was assured of extraordinary blessing…." (p. 842). The first person to write about the Pilgrimage was a Bishop of the Church in 950. I read in a book in one of the albergues (how sorry I am that I did not write the title down!) that the first Pilgrimage was completed in 885.

Spain, and specifically northern Spain, is an amazing mixture of Basque to the east (their mysterious origins and DNA are under study), Celtic in Galicia, and an extensive Moorish/Islamic influence, to name the major ones. Go way back, and we start with the earliest human remains in Europe, *Homo Antecessor*, 900,000 years old in Atapuerca which is on the Way. From there, you can find evidence of Late Paleolithic, 10,000 B.C., 30 miles off the Way. There are Megalithic remains, 4,000 B.C., in Galicia. European Celts settled in northern Spain, specifically Galicia. Rome occupied the Iberian Peninsula around 200 B.C., drawn there by mining.

The early Christian period starts in 40 A.D. It appears that St. James did actually proselytize in Spain, for which he was beheaded by Herod in 42 A.D., as stated previously. The Moors completed their invasion from North Africa by the early 700's. In 778, Charlemagne crossed the Pyrenees to stop their advances, and we get the Battle of Roncesvalles, the "Song of Roland." From the Battle of Clavijo in 844, history is witness to El Cid in the 1000's, and to the final victory battle of Las Navas de Tolosa in 1212. There were many religious and chivalrous orders, including Knights Templar, Knights of Santiago, and the Hospitallers of St. John to name a few.

Then you have the Golden Age of Isabel and Fernando, famous for sending Christopher Columbus to what would be called the Americas, as well as the infamous Inquisition and expelling the Jews from Spain. They oversaw the final demise of Islamic rule in Spain.

The Franco years, 1936-1975, bring us into our age. The bloody civil war from 1936-1939 still casts its shadow on the country. You pass deeply moving memorials of this tragic and recent time on El Camino.

Michener call's León's cathedral "a symphony of windows." (p. 871). Gaudí's bishop's palace in Astorga is magical, fanciful, and grandiose and now serves as a fabulous museum for The Way of St. James. O'Cebreiro has stone buildings with thatched roofs that are unchanged since early Celtic (yes, Celtic) times. These are just three random examples of extraordinary places you see on The Way that touched me deeply. At every stop, you could spend weeks, months, years comprehending the history and culture. I also did the little walk several kilometers off the Way to a treasure of a Romanesque Church, Vilar de Donas. Sitting quietly by myself, I was enchanted.

I was moved by the ancient octagonal church in Torres del Rio, and I am sorry I didn't walk the extra miles to see the Monastery in Samos. Once home to 1100 monks, there are now about 18 living there.

Spanish legend says that the Milky Way was formed by the dust of walking Pilgrims.

The first travel guide book in the history of the world might be the *Codex Calixtinus*. It is also called the *Liber Sancti Jacobi, the Book of Saint James*. It is a 12th century illuminated manuscript and the earliest known copy of it, from 1150, is in the Cathedral in Santiago de Compostela. It was stolen in 2011 and retrieved unharmed in 2012. Book I is the liturgies. Book II is about Miracles. Book III is about St. James's body getting from Jerusalem to Galicia. Pilgrims gathered scallop shells as souvenirs along the Galician coast and that partially explains how they became a symbol representing St. James. Book IV is about Charlemagne and the Battle of Roncevaux Pass in 778, as well as the death of his nephew, Roland, in battle. Book V is the travel guide portion, filled with advice for the Pilgrim along the Way – where to stay, what to avoid, what to see, and a guide to Santiago de Compostela. (All of the information in this paragraph is from Wikipedia).

Here is a good place to quote from Millán Bravo Lozano's book (*A Practical Guide for Pilgrims: The Road to Santiago)* about just three of the many (I repeat, many) stunning churches and cathedrals.

"Torres del Río is the location of one of the architectural jewels of the Spanish stretch of the Camino de Santiago: the octagonal Romanesque Church of the Holy Sepulchre, which features a semi-circular apse, a round tower and a lantern crowning the main cupola. (Lanterns such as this acted as beacons to guide pilgrims to their destination.) Unfortunately, the church's origins are undocumented, although these unusual Romanesque octagonal churches…are usually linked to the Templars order due to their similarity to the octagonal Church of the Holy Sepulchre in Jerusalem, which was under the protection of the Knights Templars for many years. Their exoticism, added to their obscure origins, has led them to be associated, perhaps wrongly, with the mysterious and unexplained sudden disappearance of the Templar Order." (82)

"There are few documented Templar institutions along the pilgrims' way, but one of them is to be found at Villalcázar de Sirga…with the clear vocation of protecting the pilgrims' route. All that remains of the magnificent Templar installations is the impressive 13th-century Church of Santa María la Blanca. This transitional Romanesque construction is built in the shape of a Latin cross, with a three-aisles, ribbed-vaulted nave and a double crossing, and has an enormously tall porch framing a richly carved portal." (140)

"After passing through Eirexe and Portos, a small detour takes you to Vilar de Donas, the site of the most outstanding small Romanesque church of the twenty or more specimens to be found in the Palas de Rei area. The first reference to the Church of El Salvador dates from 1184, when it was taken over by the Knights of the Order of St. James. From then on, it became the Order's official burial place in Galicia. The church nevertheless appears to have had its origins two centuries earlier when Don Arias de Monterros and his wife founded a nunnery there….The church is classified as a national monument….(220)

Chapter 11

SEMPER GUMBY: AN ATTITUDE OF GRATITUDE

Wisdom is learning to recognize beforehand what ought to work.
~author unknown

Shortly before I left on the Pilgrimage, I read a book called *Imperial Grunts*. The author, Robert Kaplan, interviewed a Marine who jokingly told him that the real motto of the Marine Corps was "Semper Gumby," always flexible, always ready. I decided to make Semper Gumby my motto on the Pilgrimage. In retrospect, it was one of the best thing I did for myself and it was life-changing. Here's how.

First of all, I love the little cartoon character, Gumby, and his sidekick, the horse, Pokey. Gumby brings a smile to my face just looking at him or saying his name. Secondly, it's an important way to live, being flexible and having a good attitude and it was even more vital on El Camino.

As I was preparing to leave home, I knew that it was going to be hard work, this Pilgrimage. I had no idea what it would be like to be with all sorts of Pilgrims under a variety of conditions. I didn't even know what the conditions were! I didn't know if I had what it took to walk the whole Way. You get tired, you get cranky, people irritate you.

You ache. You're annoyed. You end up in a place that isn't 100 per cent to your liking. Someone says something or does something irritating. There's a line for the showers. You can't do your laundry. Someone's using nail polish remover in the bunk room. Someone leaves the door open that needs to be shut (over and over and over again, this one). An incident rubs you the wrong way. On and on goes the list of potential aggravations. And then, Wait! Those are circumstances. That's just life happening in a microcosm. I quickly learned to step back, take a deep breath, and work to see every negative in some positive light.

If I had to wait, it gave me the opportunity to do something useful with the time. If I was annoyed with someone, I eventually turned it into reflection and figured out a way to say something positive. Here is the most telling example of it.

I was bound and determined to walk every step of the Way and do it wearing my backpack. I was not going to get a ride for even five, ten, or twenty kilometers. However much my back ached and my feet hurt, I was not going to ship my backpack to the next albergue, ever. The only way I could say that I had walked the whole Way with my backpack was to be 100% about it. The farther I walked, the prouder and more righteous I felt about it. The more righteous I felt, the more I kind of looked down my nose at Pilgrims who took cabs or buses part of the Way or shipped their backpack forward to their next Albergue.

There is the ever-present challenge of getting those 12-20 miles accomplished each day. Sometimes I dragged myself into an albergue. One day was particularly memorable. The approach to Portomarín is a long single-lane foot bridge separated from traffic that crosses a river that has a dam to create a reservoir. I was exhausted that day and was relieved to think that when I finished with the bridge, the town was right there and I would find an albergue immediately. Wrong! As I stepped onto the ground from the bridge, there in front of me were, unavoidably, about 120 of the steepest, most worn stone steps that I have ever seen in my life. I stopped dead in my tracks and felt like crying. There were no hand rails so I did what I had to do – fairly crawled up them at a snail's pace, knowing that at least when I got to the top, the town was right there. Wrong! Another long mildly steep hill took me eventually to my albergue.

The prouder I felt about what I was accomplishing, the more determined I became. There was only one day that I wondered if I could do it and it was when I was walking after an awful night of food poisoning (I am sparing you the details, gentle reader). Even then I didn't think for a moment of getting a cab or catching the bus. I simply wondered whether I should stop for another day of rest. I decided not to. Carry on, was my motto, however slowly, and stop short for the day if need be.

It's funny how life works. Focus on the negative and you don't have room for the positive. Spend time in those dark thoughts and it gets in the way of being in the moment. It colors your ability to see people for who they are with their own struggles. Truly, on this Pilgrimage you are surrounded by fascinating people from everywhere in the world – all ages, races, genders. You are walking through magnificent countryside. History embraces you. That's what matters. Leave the rest behind.

I was about three-quarters of the way to Santiago de Compostela, it had been a long uphill day, and I was feeling good. I was tired and energized at the same time. Recently a fellow Pilgrim had reminded me that I had my Way and other Pilgrims had theirs. Their walks were theirs and they had the right to do it their way. Still, I felt pretty darned good that I had made it this far, and every day closer to Santiago de Compostela made it more likely that I would complete the Pilgrimage.

On this day, I stepped out of a wonderful little bar having enjoyed a vegetable power drink and a carrot ginger cookie. It was perfection! I had one more hill to climb before I reached the next town and my albergue. As I came out into the afternoon sunshine, a taxi van was pulling up and a couple a little older than myself stepped out. They paid the driver, looked at me, and the wife said to her husband in what sounded like a snide voice, "Aren't you glad we aren't wearing HER backpack." Oh! Those were exactly the wrong words for my righteous self to hear. Here was a perfect afternoon and they came along and spoiled it. As I started walking, I put my tongue in the pencil sharp-ener and thought about a sufficient retort. I felt utterly offended by her comment.

The next hour of walking was difficult – the Way was steep and uneven, and I was fuming about what I had overheard and how I was going to respond. It's funny, though, this reflecting on the meaning of the Pilgrimage. They were ahead of me and she was having a hard go of it. I started thinking about how ungenerous it was for me to have these super-negative thoughts. I was still annoyed as could be, yet my fume was being replaced by introspection, by wondering what her circumstances were. As I caught up to her, I found myself saying, much to my surprise, "You look like you are struggling. What can I do to help?" I was shocked when those words came out of my mouth. She proceeded to thank me and then the conversation began. She told me about how she'd had a partial knee replacement six months earlier and it had failed, making this particular hill a torture. She was having the partial replaced in a couple of months and was scheduling the other knee for full replacement the following year. It turned out that she and her husband had walked the entire Camino decades ago, beginning in St. Jean Pied de Port, and they were doing this section to remind them-selves of that past glory and relive the experience while they both still could. We walked together for about a mile and they were delightful to talk with. I felt deep remorse even having the thoughts I had had. I did not get their names. Talk about eating humble pie. It was the most profound lesson I had about not being judgmental, not being quick to judge, and about not only embracing but also savoring every person's Way as their Way.

This sort of thing happened a lot. You'd be lost in your own thoughts walking along, you'd encounter someone and you'd start thinking about that Pilgrim, sometimes with judgment in your heart, sometimes just wondering. If it was the former, then you'd have a conversation with yourself about not being in that place, you'd soften, you'd grow to like them as you continued to encounter them. You'd also have a deep sense of loss as you spent time with fellow Pilgrims, for five or ten minutes, a day, three or four days, reencountering. Then they were gone. I had them in my heart for the rest of the journey and either rejoiced when I saw them again or felt a small burden of sadness that they were gone. A little bit of your soul goes with them.

Other times, just the right Pilgrim would give you a piece of advice or support and you'd buck up your courage and go. I was worried about the steep hill and long trek through unsupported wilderness to arrive at San Juan de Ortega. I had already walked about 5 miles that morning so I was having an internal debate as to whether I should stop at this town before the hill and face the challenging stretch the next day with an early start. Two brothers from the US were at the fountain as I filled my water bottle. When I expressed my angst out loud to them, they joked with me and then got serious said that of course I could make it. It wasn't as far as I had calculated, the only long steep part was the beginning, and they were going so they'd keep their eye out for me. It was just the push I needed and away I went. It was a spectacular day and by no means the hardest or longest.

You will play the fool. You will laugh at yourself. You will grow wiser with every step. You really will. As you pass time on the Way, you are anthropologist, listening ear, historian, journalist, adventurer, leader, follower, Pilgrim, friend. You walk hand in hand with your fears. You rejoice when you see people from past days. You struggle as likes and dislikes surface. You delve deeper with acquaintances who become friends. You spend a lot of time turning inward. You pay utmost attention to every step.

How did mild fear turn to confidence that I would complete the journey? How did everything come together so that I transformed from struggling Work in Progress with unconditioned muscles into an energized, well-oiled machine. Keep yourself open to the process. Trust yourself. Listen to your body. Struggle mightily. Laugh.

Chapter 12

KEEPING IN TOUCH

Let the important stuff in.
~Linda Lambert

I wrote four emails to family and friend in the 41 days. It was complicated and time-consuming to find a computer to send them on and there was something so inward about the Pilgrimage that I didn't worry about it. Although we hadn't planned it this way, I ended up texting my daughters frequently to give them updates and to let them know I was safe. Because they are of the moment, there is a freshness to the emails and the texts that brings this experience alive, so I am including them in full.

Texting with my daughters:

Day 11. 140 miles so far. Feel soooo good. Have met people from 23 countries! Amazing conversations. Slept in a monastery last night. Tomorrow a long day so resting up.

Probably a full rest day in Burgos or León. Today thoughts & reflections seeped in. Every day unfolds. Today was hard. First really humid. Then rainy. Then windy. I finally just packed it in. Said a sad goodbye to a wonderful Swiss guy who is now planning to do 18-20 miles a day & to a Venezuelan woman almost my age whom I've been walking with for 3 days. We cried when we realized we probably won't be walking more together. Quite incredible these connections. People really do look out for each other. Love you more than you could ever know. You are like an angel on my shoulder.

Today was by necessity 16.4 miles! No blisters, no injuries! Day by day....

Stronger by the day. The spirit of each other keeps us moving. These little conversations with you are wonderful. Am moving into countryside tomorrow. Probably less contact. Love you to bits. P.S. have seen so many adorable dogs.

Your Mother's Day Euros are treating to El Cid Hotel in Burgos, Hillary. Double bed, bathtub, total day of rest. Gracias! On the way bright & early tomorrow. Cathedral incredible inside. Managed to buy safety pins (imperdibles), sunscreen, & find & use an ATM.

Heated marble bathroom floor. What luxury for a Pilgrim? Looong delightful soak in tub. Then nap. Dinner 7:45. Look forward to being back in groove tomorrow.

Today I calculated distance done & to go. In 2 days I am halfway there! I have decided to slow my pace down from the current recommended of 15-18 miles & stay with ab't 12. It challenges me but doesn't threaten injury. Should be in León in 6 days. Every day, same friendly people & always new faces. Bunkmate tonight a Korean man who speaks excellent English. So many Koreans on el Camino this year. Fascinating. Your enthusiasm about my adventure makes my heart sing.

The towns that have albergues are more like 12-13 miles. Just the way it is. Not rushing. Want to ponder my options as I walk. Also don't know how I'll feel at the end. May be ready to just come home. May not. This in incredibly intense on many levels. Reunited over wine and dinner w/ a couple haven't seen for ten days. Magical. Templar church unbelievable.

Sent 3.8 pounds of 'what-ifs' home from León. Can't believe the useless weight I've been lugging. It'll make a huge difference!

It is unbelievable to me too! I did not know I had this endurance. It is sooo much fun! And I am really taking time to see things, appreciate beauty ar'd me, see history. Totally amazing. Your love & enthusiasm are truly a part of it.

Yesterday steep downhill. Tomorrow long uphill. It was actually an easy day. My body parts aren't complaining. Tomorrow is supposed to be steep down & gorgeous shady valley. The next day, long way up to a town related to Celts.

I've got great pictures of gory feet & taped feet. Sometimes I leave the tape on in places for 2 or 3 days. I pay great attention to each and every part of each foot. I have not had one day of pain on either foot or anywhere else that threatened to stop me or injure me. I pay close attention to this all the time.

107 more miles. Probably 9 or 10 days. Holy cow. Cutest little perro at this albergue. Took a pic of him sleeping under the table. It's so interesting the many challenges to staying fit & healthy & focused. Really fun, especially over 500 miles of attention.

I am amazed too! Feet a natural part of a whole. Finding systems that work. Lightening my load. Diligently keeping water full. Diligently sunscreening. Always always always paying attention to where I place my feet. Never ever complaining. About anything. Helping others and letting them help me. Being grateful for the hard parts. Being quiet & efficient when I leave in the morning. Trusting my own decisions and still paying close attention to what others do. Being willing to take off my pack & consult my guide when in doubt. How's that for starters?

30 countries so far! What we have in common is we are all Pilgrims having this walk. Seeking peace. Not one person has been like any other. So interesting! Unbelievable how much fun. Give & take, sometimes just a moment or the person will take the time to have a long conversation before they go back to their pace. Or the person shows back up days or weeks later. I think a Korean wrote a book that inspired Koreans much the way 'The Way' inspired Americans. As to their friendliness, it is noticeable. The other super-friendly group are the Danes. But everyone's pretty darn friendly!

32 miles to go. Should be there Monday. What a lovely day. Re-encountered the fun-loving Irish guy. Walked for an hour with the German from the albergue last night. Awesome. Saw Ivan whom I bunked with 1 day out of Roncesvalles. Now bunked in with two Swedish women one of whom works with Syrian refugees, the other of whom did a crazy tour of the West including Mt. Rushmore & Yellowstone. Gets better every day. xoxoxoHappyFeet, er mOm.

Had to choose short or very long. Short. Arzua. 22 miles to go! Should be Monday. Will text from Plaza. Can't believe it. Nothing new. Incredible. xoxoxomOm

I am in an incredible albergue 12 miles from Santiago. Tomorrow's the day! I am in a state of euphoria as well as disbelief & today was poignant. I started saying goodbye to Spain & thanking El Camino for taking good care of me & teaching me so much. Thrilled to bump into the two Swedish women so we could exchange emails. I will text you next from the Plaza! xoxoxomOm

I arrived at the church in Santiago today at 12:30. Tourists asked about my Pilgrimage & asked to take my picture. I can't quite believe I did it! Your love and enthusiasm & support made all the difference. It lasted an eternity and only a moment.

Would you two do a little research for me & see whether RyanAir can fly me from Santiago to London, to Brussels, to Barcelona & the cost for each one-way leg. May want to visit Af & Chris & Phil. May want to head home. Am starting to think about it. Thanks my sweeties. xoxoxoxomOm

And here are my emails:

Almost to Burgos

Hola Dear Daughters and Sheila, Family, Friends, Salonistas, and Renegades,

After an awesome week with Julia in Barcelona and Pamplona, we spent our last night together at my starting point in Roncesvalles. She saw the notice of the blessing in the church next to the albergue and it was moving to have the blessings of five priests in many languages, including Korean, inviting people of any and all faiths to walk El Camino in Peace, to help each other along the way, and to bring peace into the world.

Julie and I waved to each other at 7:30 a.m. (correction: it was actually 6:30) on April 22 until we couldn't see each other and away I went. Today, I completed my 11th day, averaging about 12 miles a day! It has been incredible. Scenic, historical, friendly, hard. Steep steep hills that are worse by far to come down than to go up. I am delighted with the shoes and socks I chose and also with my backpack. My minor blister issues are resolving well and I pay good attention to sunscreen, hydration, and rest. Every day my knees, hips, and feet have complained less and my endurance increases. I journal every day, write notes in my guidebook, and have taken numerous photos.

We walk through wilderness, farmland, vineyards, beside highways and roads, across medieval stone arched bridges into ancient towns. Last night I stayed in a monastery in Groñon, sleeping in the eaves of the 13th century church with fifteen other people on mats. This albergue is run by volunteers and they shop for the group to cook a shared meal and we all cooked, set tables, did dishes.

I have met people from 24 countries. Today, sadly, I said goodbye to a wonderful Swiss guy who is going to start pushing way faster than I am. I also tearily said goodbye to a Venezuelan woman, Montserrat, with whom I have shared the trail and albergues and plans for three nights.

The first day I wrote a lot of poetry in in my head and here is the haiku it inspired:

> ahead and behind
> river of pilgrims walking
> follow scallop shells

Lots of people stop somewhere because of injury. Others, usually European, come and do ten days or two weeks at a time. Some people have their bags shipped by taxi from albergue to albergue. I am committed to walking to Santiago, with my backpack on, Every Blessed Centimeter.

For a while I shared the Way with three young Korean ladies (lots and lots of Koreans on El Camino this year, which surprised me). This lively bunch, named Kim, Lim, and Areum, took a shining to me and named me their honorary grandmother. Whenever they saw me, they'd shout, Halmuhni Christy and run up and hug me. They are far ahead of me by now. I miss their energy. It is replaced by others.

Someone told me that the first two weeks are about the body - aches and pains, figuring it all out. The second two weeks are about the mind - endurance I guess, as we hit the plains. The final time is euphoria. We shall see. For now, every day brings its challenges of terrain and surface. It also brings its beauty in ancient towns, albergues, and churches, and incredibly friendly people. We all say "Buen Camino" to each other. It is touching how often people in the villages and cities also wish us Buen Camino.

The first three days, the quote Rich gave me from Thicht Nhat Han sustained me in some pretty brutal walking: "I am home, I have arrived, my destination is in each step." I tell you, this is a lesson in paying attention to each step. Each step. Each step. This is the first time I have had access to email. I hope each and everyone one of you is well. I am now a little over a quarter of the way through the journey. Isn't that amazing?! In three days I will be in Burgos which is said to have the second most stunning cathedral in Spain, after Seville.

Much love to you all,

Christy

Hola from Boadilla del Camino

I have a quick opportunity in a small town to send an email to the four of you. To say that this journey is incredible is an understatement. The walking part of it is exceedingly challenging. Lots of steep long hills, difficult walking surfaces from pebbly to clay, dirt, rock, highway. Weather hot cold, dry, rainy, windy. Each afternoon I discover where I will stay. Often a municipal albergue for 5 Euros a night. One night a 14th century monastery. Last night a five-hundred-year-old home now an albergue. Often have the Pilgrims dinner and sometimes shop and cook. The countryside is gorgeous. Through wine country where I have been drinking wine for a dollar a glass. Now farmland rich with alfalfa, oats, wheat. Every five or ten miles, we walk through another Medieval town or village or city. Everyone is exceedingly friendly to us and helpful and Pilgrims are kind and helpful with each other. Like the blessing ceremony asked us to be, remember Julie? I have now encountered and shared the way with people from 24 countries.

The mystery evolves. I take care of my feet first, then my laundry, then me. You participate in spirit. You are my angels of love and I will see you before you know it.

here is my haiku for today

> walk walk walk walk walk
> there is no way to the way
> the way is the way

Lots and lots of love,
Christy

Each one of you, dearest of dear, made this Pilgrimage possible.

Day 22

Hola Everyone,

Today was my 22nd day on El Camino de Santiago de Compostela. It is as compelling now as it was the first day. My routines are simple and center around arriving after the walk, taking care of my feet (moisturizing, taking care of latent and full blown blisters, doing jin shin on them), writing up the day in my John Brierley guide book (the only book in my pack), journaling. Then I shower, do my laundry by hand and safety pin it to the line. Life is extremely simple and satisfying. The Pilgrim dinners are sometimes fabulous and sometimes just satisfying. The fine Spanish local red wine costs 1 Euro per glass, 2.50 for the bottle.

Everyone is congenial and we weave back and forth into each other's lives. Today I prepared with a British couple for taking off early. Usually "lights on" in the albergues are 6 to 6:30. We had a 15.2 mile walk ahead of us across the meseta on the old Roman Road. It was going to be hot and difficult. We decided to leave as close to 5 as possible to get ahead of the midday heat. So as not to disturb bunkmates, we moved our readied packs out of the bunk area and into the kitchen, slept in our clothes and fled in the darkness. What was unusual about this day was that the Roman Road (literally) is unsupported by bathrooms, restaurants, fountains, albergues should you decide to stop early. Nothing but walking, which I did by myself, lost in thought. Each day is a different challenge. This one was the rough surface and I finally pulled out my walking poles to deal with it.

What an amazing bunch. You get non-judgmental and just plain accepting of everyone. Actually beyond accepting - genuinely enjoying people because they are on their own journey on El Camino. I have met people now from 25 countries. My bunkmates last night were from Hungary – Tomas, 16, and his dad, Chubba. Sometimes I am in small cubbies with four bunks, sometimes in a room with up to 60 other residents. Toilets, showers, laundry facilities vary in quality but always there. The most inspiring couple I have met are from Niagara Falls, Canada. She has MS and is walking for the cause. The huge daily struggles with terrain, footing, distance, are even greater for her. For about ten days our paths intertwined and I was always overjoyed when they appeared in the bunkroom or we sat down to Pilgrims Dinner together. Yesterday, I was walking through a small town at going-to-school time. I passed by groups of kids from elementary to high school. To a person, they called out "Buen Camino." A farmer driving his big tractor waved and called out. People on the street. It is heartwarming.

When I took El Camino on, I decided from the get-go that I would enjoy everything and that I would not complain about anything. And so it has been. At the monuments marking the way, people leave rocks big and small to leave behind concerns or express thanks for something. I have done both.

At twelve miles a day, roughly, I have fifteen more days of walking. Nothing obligates me to go that speed but it is a comfortable distance when it works. It is staggering how much history I have walked through. Too much to absorb, really, but well-covered by my guidebook, my notes, and my photos. Julia, the little Canon you gave me is fabulous! Hillary, I wouldn't have survived the sun without the hat you gave me.

Tomorrow, I should arrive in León. I will take a rest day to, well, rest, to visit the cathedral and the Gaudí cathedral, and to ship a pound and a half of stuff home. That will make my last days so much easier.

The first couple of weeks were about the body - aches, pains, blisters, tired muscles. Now it more about the mind - will power, endurance, pushing through. The last week, they say, is about euphoria. I am ready!

All of your love and friendship are with me on Camino. Carol, you and Mark would love it. Let´s talk.

Lots of love,
Christy

Almost There!

Hola Everyone!

32 miles to Santiago! I should be there on Monday! I am writing tonight because, well, first of all, I have access to a computer so I am taking advantage of it. Second of all, El Camino is turning into a sea of people and I know that when I arrive in Santiago, I might not be able to communicate.

Wow! It continues to be simply amazing on so many levels. People I saw at the very beginning; I am suddenly encountering again. Continue to walk and talk with an amazing variety of interesting people of all ages. Sarria is where many Pilgrims step onto the Way because it is just before the 100 kilometer mark after which they can get their Compostela certificate. It has turned into a bit of a party in both good ways and bad. There is not so much the group spirit as there has been and people who are just going a short distance haven´t gone through the shared struggles and pain. Fun nevertheless. The number of countries I have met Pilgrims from is up to 30.

One of the most fascinating parts of the Camino is how common our struggles are and how we support each other in them. I have definitely gone from a work in progress to a well-oiled machine. I can be up, dressed, and out the door with my backpack in five minutes in the dark without disturbing a soul. My feet are now tough and pain free and I thank them every day with a good massage and bath and a moisturizer mixed with lavender essential oil. My legs, firmly muscled up, say, Let's go! The miles roll by. My backpack (thanks in great part to you, Julia, for the big, excellent adjustment at the beginning) has now been adjusted to perfection and I hardly feel it, especially after I sent 4 pounds home from León. Everything has evolved into place for ready access, and I continue to be diligent about hydration, sunscreen and shading my eyes.

It simply astounds me that all of us are actually going through the same torture and loving it. The walking surface is often appalling. Cobbled, broken, slippery, slate surfaces. Often steep. If you go up you go down and down used to be way harder. The other day, the 13-mile day to a Celtic town called O´Cebreiro, included a five-mile stretch that was entirely uphill. I couldn't believe how great it felt!

In the evenings, over Pilgrim dinners, often lovingly prepared by the owners of the albergues and sometimes astonishingly delicious, we talk and laugh and solve all the problems of the world, including our own. I sense in each and every person, a deep desire to come back to the world with peace in our hearts. The generosity of spirit as we settle in for the night is heartwarming.

I am however going to write a story about this experience and it will include a chapter titled Muni Manners. As in Municipal Albergues. As in where we are packed in like sardines. Lemme see. Just because you and your friend are awake doesn't mean that everyone else wants to hear you start conversing. If you want to get an early start, probably a good and polite idea to pack your bag the night before, not remove everything and repack it in the morning. Your headlamp or cell phone or flashlight is not pleasant in others' eyes. I promised not to complain, ever, on El Camino, so I have learned to just accept this craziness.

So, three days from my goal and I may or may not be able to email everyone. I still can't quite believe I have walked all these miles, thought so many thoughts, processed so much emotion, feeling, struggle, and that my body, mind, and soul have loved every minute of it. I am in awe of some of the people who are finishing who have real struggles with their bodies. I plan to be able to say in two or three days that I walked every single foot of the 489 miles wearing my backpack. This perhaps sounds peculiar but in fact there are bus, taxi and private services galore to transport backpacks and Pilgrims for as much of The Way as they choose not to walk or carry their load.

One of my favorite stops was yesterday when I ended my day a bit short so I could detour off the Way and walk 2 miles to a 12th century church where the Knights of Santiago are buried. I did it by myself in the heat of the afternoon and sat quietly for a long time in the ancient space. It already stands out as one of the best afternoons on El Camino. Oh the pictures, and journaling, and notes I have!

Lots of love to you all,
Christy

Chapter 13

IN SEARCH OF MEANING

*It is good to have an end to journey toward but it is the journey
that matters in the end.*

~Ernest Hemingway

El Camino is a magnificent metaphor for life. In so many ways, this long, thoughtful Pilgrimage reflects us the way life does. It is a microcosm of our real struggles. As my friend Ryan said, El Camino really starts when you arrive in Santiago. It's when you get home that you begin to know which lessons learned will stay with you - and prepare you to accept future lessons with gratitude. Soren Kierkegaard said, "Life can only be understood backwards; but it must be lived forwards."

My daughter Julia said that for her the biggest part of my Pilgrimage was about the continuity. We talked about how fellow Pilgrims threaded in and out of the days. We talked about how Pilgrims have walked this path for 1300 years, how I was constantly walking someone else's footsteps. The river of Pilgrims walking in the same direction provided a companionable togetherness. And yet I was often happily alone and lost in my own thoughts. You will feel brave and scared at the same time and you will encounter your own wisdom and your own foolishness. We create our own Pilgrimage and it was created by interaction with fellow Pilgrims.

My daughter Hillary was moved by my Semper Gumby attitude and especially wanted me to write about gratitude. Iris Apfel said that all you need is curiosity and a sense of humor. That seems fitting on El Camino, especially to laugh at your own foibles.

I think of many people who touched me on the Way, and I them. Here is a small sampling: Jacob and Louise and her living with MS were inspiring in their deep faith and love. Monce felt like a sister as our friendship deepened for three lovely days. I defended Ryan's and my using a frying pan from predation by a fellow Pilgrim cooking at the Albergue. Ivan with terrible blisters from the passage over the Pyrenees had immediate need of my container of Vaseline, which I gladly gave him, not knowing at the time whether I would need it myself and could replace it. Doroty needed comfort -and her water bottle filled and some snacks - when she was sick and in turn gave me my first Compeed bandages. An afternoon of talking and drinking nothing short of divine hot chocolate with Giuliano was magical and then we partook of a Galician Quaimada ceremony in the evening. I had an engaging after-dinner conversation with Georg who wanted me to fill him in about anti-Viet Nam war days and we had a lengthy conversation about how 3D printing is changing the world. I watched Austin, architect and now treasured friend, doing one of his incredible pen and ink drawings. How touching it was to say goodbye to fellow Pilgrims, feeling certain I'd never see them again as they forged ahead faster, only to encounter them in a later town or at the end in Santiago de Compostela.

What gave me the courage to do it by myself? How did the Pilgrimage transform me? What did I discover about religion, spirituality, self? Those are enormous questions. Transformation unfolds and you don't realize until later that you are different. These are not easily answered. Here goes.

There will be times when you are walking that your spirit is awakened and the universe pauses to let you be in that moment. Such was that hour that I sat in utter solitude and damp silence in the quiet dark church, Vilar de Donas, and I felt the monumental meaning of the Pilgrimage. The best you can do is be as fully in the moment as possible and keep good records – journaling, notes, photos, so that when you return and process your experience – a lifetime endeavor for sure – you can deepen your memory and be able to share it meaningfully with others. It would be impossible to see it all, understand it all, and appreciate every detail. You barely scratch the surface. When you get back, you will wish there had been more hours in each day, more energy in your tired body, and more awareness in the moment of just how extraordinary each place was. In some amazing way, we truly do become ourselves more deeply as we walk this Pilgrimage.

A sign in Hornillos said "Keep walking though there's no place to get to. Don't try to see through the distance. That is not for human beings. Move within…." The first couple of weeks are about the body and stamina. The second two weeks are about the mind and determination. The rest of the Way is about euphoria, anticipation, and yes, possibly, rapture. It will take every ounce of what you have. You will dedicate yourself, sometimes seriously and sometime in the most absurd ways, to overcoming your own weakness, to staying committed. It takes mindfulness and courage. At some moment on the Way, something new opens in your mind and body. You know, at last, that you will finish your Pilgrimage. You know it is fun. You know it is more than struggle. You are transformed. You let the joy in! "When you walk, arrive at every step." (Thicht Nhat Han). Arriving at every step keeps you grounded in that very moment, that step, that minute.

I remember one specific day, as I stepped out of the Albergue at 6 a.m., it was as if my legs said to me: we're on it today. You don't have to worry about us anymore. How fast do you want to go? It was incredible. My body reflected the change. When I returned home and had a follow-up medical exam, physically, my body had toned up, I lost 40 pounds, my cholesterol plummeted, blood sugar went back to normal. And I now go for a walk every single day.

I was witness to profound faith, devotion, and kindness that moved me. I was touched that so many religions, along with the non-theists, walked in peace, wanted to learn from each other and inspire each other. Kindness prevailed in little moments of thoughtfulness to big acts of kindness. One of my Pilgrim friends, when I caught up with him later, had developed a severe infection in one of his feet. Pharmacists in Spain, rather than doctors, are your first resource. The pharmacist took one look at his foot, feared potential sepsis and immediately called an ambulance and proceeded to walk with him the 4 miles to where an ambulance could take him to the hospital for a long stay and successful healing.

People often seem surprised and they think I am courageous to have walked El Camino de Santiago de Compostela by myself. It did not feel like an act of courage. I live alone and, as much as I love doing things with friends and family, I love doing things by myself as well. This Pilgrimage was said to be well-supported and indeed it was! Finding your pace is hard and I suspect that it was easier for me than it was for someone with a friend or a spouse. I was also pretty much on my own to dig deep to overcome some of the physical challenges and exhaustion. I saw some contentious interactions between friends and couples that at times made me glad I was on my own. Right here is a salute to Jacob and Louise – the only couple I saw on the entire El Camino who loved to walk holding hands and often did. What an inspiration you were!

Being by myself allowed me to be utterly flexible and comfortable about when and where to stop to eat, to rest, to spend the night. I had enough internal debate going on, never mind deciding with someone else. When you travel alone, I think you also get more full and direct contact with others. I found the connections I made to be rich, warm, and rewarding. There was also a kindness and thoughtfulness directed at me by fellow Pilgrims and by those who served me that was born of respect for an elder. That was inspiring and heartwarming. Though people shared their religious thoughts when asked, not once did I feel like someone was trying to bend me to their religious beliefs. That includes the priests and nuns.

I came home renewed in a faith in humankind and a huge desire to do my part to bring peace and justice to the world. Though the Pilgrimage did not make me religious, it did make me profoundly respectful of others' religions. It also made me fierce about being willing to be myself, to be authentic, to confront my own fears, and, yes, to laugh at myself. I wanted to be open-minded to others and I wanted to be kind.

I became more mindful of paying attention to others' needs on The Way, to give of my spirit freely, to embrace each person for their individuality. It also made me kinder and more patient with myself. Sometimes it was hard. Sometimes I felt silly or absurd. Other times I felt bossy. Sometimes I wanted to tell someone off. I only did it once and it felt shameful. It was easy to give up selfishness because we looked out for each other. Whenever I needed to bite my tongue, I'd say to myself, "Semper Gumby" and it would make me smile and give my reactions some breathing room. It worked!

I had a wonderful conversation with Sister Monica, a Benedictine nun in León. She had given the Pilgrim blessing the night before and spoke seven languages fluently. She reminded me that each and every one of us is on a Camino our whole life. We never stop searching for meaning. She said people often suggested to her that it must be easy for her, the path she chose, that she didn't need to struggle with meaning now that she was a nun. She said it was quite the opposite, that, if anything, it deepened her struggle. She told me about her time in a student teaching position in St. Louis, working with impoverished black kids. What an amazing human being she was. I am grateful I had the chance to talk with her.

Rick Davis, R.I.P. dear one, said "Observe and absorb." That is truly what El Camino de Santiago de Compostela is about, observing and absorbing.

I met Christians, Buddhists, Daoists, Hindus, Jews, Muslims, non-theists, Shintoists, yogis, and probably other faiths, too. I didn't ask everyone. Christians came from many different churches. Catholic were of course the predominant group on El Camino. The depth of faith and belief varied widely. What did not vary was the engaging conversations. Comfortably, politely, quickly, it seemed like each and every Pilgrim was eager to talk about their own life struggles, what brought them to El Camino, the meaning behind it, and answer any question asked. Peripatetic conversation was the best. We all felt free to engage in brief conversations, linger, or move on if the pace wasn't compatible.

Harvard did a longitudinal study about lifetime happiness and found that the key to happiness over the long haul is being comfortable, joyful, effective, and connected. El Camino reflects this magnificently.

In a homily in May of 2013, Pope Francis said, in part, "And we all have a duty to do good. And this commandment for everyone to do good, I think, is a beautiful path towards peace. If we, each doing our own part, if we do good to others, if we meet there, doing good, and we go slowly, gently, little by little, we will make that culture of encounter: We need that so much. We must meet one another doing good."

This is not so very different from what A. J. Muste said: "There is no way to peace. Peace is the way."

To make an end is to make a beginning.
~T.S. Elliot

BIBLIOGRAPHY

Brierley, John. *A Pilgrim's Guide to the Camino de Santiago:
St. Jean – Roncesvalle – Santiago.* Forres, Scotland: Camino
Guides, 2014.

Lozano, Millán Bravo. *A Practical Guide for Pilgrims: The Road to
Santiago.* León: Editorial Everest, S.A. Eighth Edition, 1999.

Luard, Elisabeth. *Classic Spanish Cooking: Recipes for Mastering the
Spanish Kitchen.* London: Octopus Publishing GroupLtd.,
2008.

Michener, James A. *Iberia.* New York: Random House, Inc., 1968.

americanpilgrims.org

Brochures along The Way.

National Geographic.

Yankee Magazine.

Wikipdia.

Write-ups from displays in León Museum.

Gratitude

You have to carry your own burden but you can't do it
without your community.

~Martin Sheen

Hillary and Julia: no finer daughters on Planet Earth. Sheila. My parents, bless their souls. Africa. Celso and Mercedes. Dear extended family. Winnie: you teach me mindfulness & kindness. Paula. Linda. Susan. Barb & Connie. Ruslyn. Rebecca. Salonista Soul Sisters. Renegade Book Group: you rock. WCE. Every single friend and family member near and dear and scattered around the world: thank you for friendship, love, advice, support, affection, humor, and inspiration. Thanks for believing in me. Eastern Mountain Sports. americanpilgrims.org. John Brierley for lighting the way. And to all of my friends, named and unnamed, on El Camino. We shared the journey, we learned from each other. You are all in my heart. Alphabetically: Anna. Austin. Chris & Angela. Chris & Steve. Dave & Bill. Daya. Doroty. Elizabet. Gary. Georg. Georgia. Glenn. Giuliano. Ivan. Jacob & Louise. Jerry. Jim. Jytta & Majbritt. Kenth. Kim, Lim & Areum. Malin & Gunvor. Marianne. Monce. Monica. Nam. Natasha & Francal. Pak. Ryan. Sebastian. Stepe. Tomas & Chubba. Walter. All the other Pilgrims unnamed who were part of my journey and I part of yours. I treasure and need the love, enthusiasm, and support of each and every one of you. I thank my lucky stars we are on this journey together. Buen Camino.

NOTES

NOTES

The author can be reached at daychristy132@gmail.com

CPSIA information can be obtained
at www.ICGtesting.com
Printed in the USA
BVHW040312210220
572972BV00005B/610